Credit Repair Kit

Credit Repair Kit

Carlos Santana

Library of Congress Control Number:		2014901510
ISBN:	Hardcover	978-1-4633-7640-6
	Softcover	978-1-4633-7639-0
	Ebook	978-1-4633-7638-3

To order additional copies of this book, please contact:
Palibrio LLC
1663 Liberty Drive
Suite 200
Bloomington, IN 47403
Toll Free from the U.S.A 877.407.5847
Toll Free from Mexico 01.800.288.2243
Toll Free from Spain 900.866.949
From other International locations +1.812.671.9757
Fax: 01.812.355.1576
orders@palibrio.com
523460

CONTENTS

INTRODUCTION

What are you going to find in this book? You will find the following tools and advise as to how to deal with your creditor in order to reestablish your credit:

1. How to negotiate with your Creditors

2. What to say and what to do

3. Sample of letters that you need to write to your Creditors

4. How to negotiate cancellation of debts

5. Requisition of Credit Bureau Report

6. Who and where to call or write

7. Synopsis of consumer protection laws.

CHAPTER I

CREDIT REPAIR KIT – THE BOOK

We all know how you got involved in the credit line business. Now let's talk about how to get out of the situation of credit loss.

In the first place it took you a long time to establish your credit lines, including personal loans, credit cards, car loan, mortgages and whatever. Now we must embark in a trip to reestablish your credit after it has been damaged.

You must be willing and able to discuss how you got there by either doing it in writing or in person. It will take you sometime to present yourself to the different companies and banks that allowed you to have their confidence and gave their monies to you. You must call these people, companies and banks and request appointments or write to them. But before you do that you must request a copy of your credit bureau report at your local office. PLEASE do not request one of these fly by night reports that are offered in the web, they will only offer your info to other credit companies.

Now that you have your appointments with different companies and credit report in hand you will write or schedule an appointment to discuss your situation with the officer in charge of your case.

CREDIT REPAIR ORGANIZATIONS ACT

This book needs additional citations for verification. Please help improve this book by adding citations from reliable sources. Without source material may be challenged and removed.

The Credit Repair Organizations Act ("CROA") is not actually an Act. It is Title IV of The Consumer Credit Protection Act. Section 401 states, however, it can be referred to as "Credit Repair Organization Act".

Now more than ever consumers must establish and maintain strong credit worthiness and standing in order to obtain more credit. As a result, many consumers who have experienced credit problems seek assistance from credit repair organizations. Some credit repair organizations, however, advertise and engage in unfair business practices which result in financial hardship for consumers, particularly those of limited economic means or those who are uneducated.

Self-respect is a condition where psychologically and economically one needs to develop oneself to be able to handle yourself in order to succeed in this society and economy. To be able to acquire the things and services one need to exist in this society we are going to need some sort of credit line if we do not have sufficient income or cash flow where more than 80% of the population will have to use

CREDIT. **YES**, credit is the only vehicle to acquire the things we need to exist and succeed in this society if you fall in the 80% of the population. To develop credit lines and banking services to your benefit to have self-respect and the respect of others, you must learn how to develop and sustain this benefit. (credit). By the following standards you will be able to acquire the ability to purchase the things you need and become successful:

† Sufficient Income
† Ability to pay
† Stability (work more than 6 months)
† Payment of utilities (water, electric bills, etc.)
† Positive payment history
† Positive ID

The purposes of the Credit Repair Organizations Act is to ensure that prospective buyers credit repair services from credit repair organizations are provided with the necessary information to make an informed decision. It intends to protect the public from unfair or deceptive advertising and business practices by credit repair organizations. It enumerates prohibited practices, required disclosures, contract requirements, liability and penalties for non-compliance and procedure to report non- compliance. The statute was signed by the President on September 30, 1996.

One of the most important areas covered by CROA is how credit repair organizations can get paid. It is the general consensus that a credit repair company can only be paid after services have been rendered. This can be done using a monthly fee model where companies charge clients on a monthly basis after services are rendered or on the more modern pay after deletion model where clients only pay after items are deleted from the credit report. Companies that charge excess "setup" fees or all of their fees upfront violate the provision of CROA.

Doing what's best for one self is the most appropriate thing to do so lets get going. You need to evaluate your finances, because you need to know where you are standing. First you add all your income sources. Then you must know what your liabilities are. Since you got into a financial situation where you are at the risk of going bankrupt, the least you can do is know where you stand.

When you learn exactly where you stand, you will be able to negotiate the elimination of you debts. You will be able to appreciate the knowledge acquired by doing a simple Income and Expense Statement of your situation. You will have the confidence to negotiate the elimination of your debts, and at the end of the month you will have some money left, hallelujah!!!

CREDIT REPAIR KIT

Following is a list of documents you may need to accomplish the task of reestablishing you credit. In order to make a good impression you will need:

1. Recent Credit Report
2. Recent pay stubs (evidence of income)
3. Evidence of unemployment, divorce, accident or death certificate
4. Bankruptcy discharge
5. Other Income, etc.
6. Attorney statements

CREDIT REPAIR SCAMS

Credit Repair – Help Yourself

You see the advertisements in newspapers, on TV and on the Internet. You hear them on the radio. You get fliers in the mail. You may even get calls from telemarketers offering credit repair services. They all make the same claims:

"Credit problems? No problem!"

"We can erase your bad credit – 100% guaranteed." "Create a new credit identity – legally."
"We can remove bankruptcies, judgments, liens and bad loans from your credit file forever."

Do yourself a favor and save some money, too. Don't believe these statements. Only time, a
conscious effort and a personal debt repayment plan will improve your credit report.

The following explains how you can improve your credit worthiness and lists legitimate resources for low or no-cost help.

CREDIT REPAIR COMPANIES

Regulations of Credit Repair Organizations

Everyday companies nationwide appeal to consumers with poor credit histories. They promise, for a fee, to clean up your credit report so you can get a car loan, a home mortgage, insurance or even a job. The truth is they can't deliver. After you pay them hundreds or thousands of dollars in up-front fees, these companies do nothing to improve your credit report; man simply vanish with your money.

THE WARNING SIGNS

If you decide to respond to a credit repair offer, beware of companies that:

† Want to pay for credit repair services before any services are provided
† Do not tell you your legal rights and what you can do – yourself – for free
† Recommend you not to contact a credit bureau directly; or
† Advise you to dispute all information in your credit report or take any action that seems illegal, such as creating a new identity. If you follow illegal advice and commit fraud, you may be subject to prosecution.

You could be charged and prosecuted for mail or wire fraud if you use the mail or telephone to apply credit and provide false information. It's a federal crime to make false statements on a loan or credit application, to misrepresent your Social Security Number and to obtain an Employer Identification Number from the Internal Revenue Service under false pretenses.

Thanks to the new Telemarketing Sales Rule, it's also a crime for telemarketers who offer credit repair services to require you to pay until six months after they've delivered the services.

THE TRUTH

No one can legally remove accurate and timely negative information from a credit report. But the law does allow you to request a reinvestigation of information in your file that you dispute as inaccurate or incomplete. There is no charge for this. Everything a credit repair clinic can do for you legally, you can do for yourself at little or no cost. According to the Fair Credit Report Act:

†   You are entitled to a free copy of your credit report if you've been denied credit within the last 30 days.

†   If your application for credit, insurance or employment is denied because of information supplied by a credit bureau, the company you applied to must provide you with that credit bureau's name and address.

†   You can dispute mistakes or outdated items for free. Ask the credit reporting agency for a dispute form or submit your dispute in writing along with any supporting documentation. Clearly identify each item in the report that you are disputing, explain why you dispute the information and request an investigation.

†   If the new investigation reveals an error, you may ask that a corrected version of the report be sent to anyone who received your report within the past six months. Job applicants can have corrected reports sent to anyone who received a report for employment purposes during the past two years.

If the reinvestigation does not resolve your dispute, have the credit bureau include your version of the dispute (up to 100 words) in your file and in future reports. Remember, there is no charge for a reinvestigation.

REPORTING NEGATIVE INFORMATION

Accurate negative information generally can be reported for seven years, but there are exceptions:

✓   Bankruptcy information can be reported for 10 years
✓   Information reported because of an application for a job with a salary of more than $75,000 has no time limitation.

DO-IT-YOURSELF CHECK-UP

Even if you don't have a poor credit history, it's a good idea to conduct your own credit check-up.

If you are planning a major purchase, such as a home or car, you may want to get copies of your credit report to ensure that the information is correct. Banks, mortgage brokers and other lenders will often look at your credit history to determine whether or not to lend your money.

Therefore, checking in advance on the accuracy of the information in your credit report could speed the credit-granting process.

Mistakes on your credit report can happen. These mistakes could be simple clerical errors or confusion among family names. For example, information may be unintentionally mixed up on the reports of family members who share the same name, such as fathers and sons.

Since negative information stays on your report for seven years, it is especially important to notify credit bureaus immediately if you suspect an error. Remember, you have the right to challenge any inaccurate or outdated information.

IDENTIFY and CORRECT errors on your credit report:

- Check your credit report once a year to check for inaccuracies.
- Check your credit report well in advance if you intend to finance a major purchase, or if you plan to apply for a mortgage or car loan.
- Report errors to both the credit bureau and to the creditor by sending a WRITTEN explanation of your dispute. Both the credit bureau and the creditor must investigate.
- If your dispute is not resolved you may ask the credit bureau to include a statement of the dispute in their files and in future reports.
- Information concerning a lawsuit or a judgment against you can be reported for seven years or until the statute of limitations runs out, whichever is longer; and
- Default information concerning U.S. Government insured or guaranteed student loans can be reported for seven years after certain guarantor actions.

CREDIT COUNSELING

Professional assistance may be just what you need to manage your debt.

If you are having trouble paying your bills or if you can't resolve your credit problems yourself, you may want to contact a credit counselor.

Credit counselors also known as "debt adjusters", are non-profit organizations that are required to be licensed in the U.S. They try to arrange repayment plans that are acceptable to you and your creditors and can also help you set up a realistic budget. The Department of Banking regulates organizations that are licensed to conduct debt adjustment activity. A list of these organizations may be found on our Web site.

Example: Consumer Credit Counseling

Licensed debt adjusters may receive your money and disburse such money to consumer creditors on your behalf. Most debt adjusters also offer counseling for persons faced with significant debt or bankruptcy, money management advice and assistance in establishing debt repayment plans and budgets.

For further information feel free to contact the Department of Banking. SELF-HELP MAY BE THE BEST
Everything a credit repair clinic can do for you legally, you can do for yourself at little or no cost.

The law allows you to request an investigation of information in your file that you may dispute as inaccurate or incomplete. There is no charge for this. According to the Fair Credit Reporting Act:

†   You are entitled to a free copy of your credit report if you've been denied credit, insurance or employment within the last 60 days. If your application for credit, insurance or employment is denied because of information supplied by a credit bureau, the company you applied to must provide you with that credit bureau's name address and telephone number. You must provide the credit bureau the letter of denial from the company or bank.

†   You can dispute mistakes or outdated items for free. Ask the credit reporting agency for a dispute form or submit your dispute in writing, along with any supporting documentation. Do not send them original documents.

†   Clearly identify each item in your report that you dispute, explain why you dispute the information and request a reinvestigation. If the new investigation reveals an error, you may ask that a

corrected version of the report be sent to anyone who received your report within the past six months. Job applicants can have can have corrected reports sent to anyone who received a report for employment purposes during the past two years.

† When the reinvestigation is complete, the credit bureau must give you the written results and a free copy of your report if the dispute results in a change. If an item is changed or removed, the credit bureau cannot put the disputed information back in your file unless the information provider verifies its accuracy and completeness, and the credit bureau gives you a written notice that includes the name, address and phone number.

† You also should tell the creditor or other information or other information provider in writing that you dispute an item. Many providers specify an address for disputes. If the provider then reports the item to any credit bureau, it must include a notice of your dispute. In addition, if you are correct – that is, if the information is inaccurate – the information provider may not use it again.

Contact the Department of Banking (In Puerto Rico Hacienda) if you need assistance regarding your dispute.

HOW TO OBTAIN COPIES OF YOUR CREDIT REPORT

As of September 1, 2005 United States residents are entitled to a free credit report once a year.

The Federal Trade Commission (FTC) amended the Fair Credit Reporting Act by requiring that the three nationwide consumer reporting agencies – Equifax, Experian and Trans Union – provide to consumers, upon their request, a free copy of their credit report once every 12 months. In the U.S. this legislation took effect on September 1, 2005.

The three companies have set up a central web site, toll-free number and mailing address through which you can order your free credit report:

Visit: annualcreditreport.com

Call toll-free: 1-877-322-8228

Mail completed Annual Credit report Request form to: Annual credit Report Request Service
P.O. Box 105281
Atlanta, GA 30348-5281

CHAPTER II

The U.S. Department of Housing and Urban Development (HUD) is pleased to provide you with information about the Emergency Homeowners' Loan Program (EHLP). Attached you will find the Pre-Applicant Screening Worksheet to determine if you might qualify for emergency assistance under the EHLP. The attached Pre-Applicant Screening Worksheet along with a signed Third Party Authorization form must be submitted to a participating counseling agency by July 22, 2011.

EHLP was created to help homeowners who are temporarily and involuntarily unemployed or underemployed due to economic conditions or a medical condition and are at risk of foreclosure. The EHLP will provide eligible homeowners with emergency assistance that pays a portion of their monthly mortgage payment for up to twenty for up to twenty-four consecutive months, or up to $50,000, whichever occurs first. Please, thoroughly read the Frequently Asked Questions and the document checklist

Demand for EHLP emergency assistance is expected to be extremely high. If necessary and to ensure a fair selection process, homeowners with eligible Pre-Application Screening Worksheets may be entered in a random lottery. Homeowners selected through the lottery will be contacted and scheduled for an appointment to complete a full EHLP application. During the application appointment, the homeowner MUST submit all documents specified under the attached Document Checklist in order for the housing counseling agent to determine his or her eligibility for program assistance. Any homeowner who fails to meet this requirement may lose his or her application position due to an incomplete application package. In that case, the next homeowner on the waiting list will be considered for formal EHLP application submission. Housing counseling agencies in participating states will be identified to accept the complete Pre-Applicant Screening Worksheet required by HUD. There is no cost to the homeowner to submit the screening worksheet. Participating housing counseling agencies can answer program questions and assist homeowners with compiling the necessary documents to submit a formal EHLP application. However, only HUD will make final eligibility determinations and final decisions about the amount and duration of a homeowners EHLP emergency assistance.

CHAPTER III

BANKRUPTCY

If you are filing or involved in a bankruptcy case and do not have an attorney, the web site of the bankruptcy court where the case has been or will be filed, may be of assistance. The Bankruptcy Resources page may be of help as well.

FORECLOSURE

Homeowners who are having trouble or have fallen behind in making their mortgage payments may have options that would allow them to avoid foreclosure and bankruptcy. For more information, check these foreclosure resources.

Beware of offers made once your house is in foreclosure – there are a number of fraudulent schemes specifically directed at individuals facing foreclosure. Contact your state attorney general or other state consumer protection agency regarding any suspicious proposal, such as one that requires transferring your property to a third party in order to avoid foreclosure.

PETITION PREPARERS

Beware of bankruptcy petition preparers who do not comply with all legal requirements. The role of non-attorney petition preparers is solely to type information on Bankruptcy Forms. Petition preparers are barred by law from providing legal advice – they cannot explain how to answer legal questions or assist in bankruptcy court. Petition preparers must sign all documents they prepare; print their name, address and social security number on such documents and furnish copies to the debtor. They cannot sign a document on the debtor's behalf or receive payment from the debtor for court fees.

Set out on Form B200 (pdf), one of the Director's Procedural Forms). The judge can also deny the discharge of all debts if a debtor does something dishonest in connection with the bankruptcy case such as destroying or hiding property, falsifying record, or lying. Individual bankruptcy cases are randomly audited to determine the accuracy, truthfulness, and completeness of the information that the debtor is required to provide. Please be aware that bankruptcy fraud is a crime.

Pro se litigants, whether debtor or creditor, are expected to follow the rules that govern procedures in the federal courts. Pro se litigants should be familiar with the United States Bankruptcy Code, the Federal Rules of Bankruptcy Procedure and the local rules of the court in which the case is filed. Local rules, along with the useful information are usually posted on the court's web site and are available at the local court's intake counter.

CREDIT COUNSELING

Individual debtors are generally required to obtain credit counseling from an approved provider within 180 days before filing a case and to file a statement of compliance and a certificate of credit counseling furnished by the provider. Failure to do so may result in dismissal of the case.

FINDING AN ATTORNEY, INCLUDING FREE LEGAL SERVICES

Debtors are strongly encouraged to obtain the services of competent legal counsel. Even if you cannot afford to pay attorney or about free (also known as "pro bono") legal services, contact your state or local bar association. May law schools have legal clinics that offer free legal services? Court web sites often have contact information for bar associations and pro bono legal service programs, as well as important procedural information.

For information about such legal resources, check the American Bar Association's Legal Help (In Puerto Rico Colegio de Abogados) page, the Legal Services Corporation or the web site of the bankruptcy court where you intend to file. If you do not know where you are permitted to file a case, check the Official Bankruptcy Forms page to see the box on Form B1 (Voluntary Petition) entitled "Information Regarding the Debtor-Venue" and the part of the Instructions relating to that box.

Appointment of Counsel Probation and Pretrial Services Jury Service Case Management / Electronic Case Files

Glossary of legal Terms

Publications and Reports

Home > Federal Courts > Bankruptcy > Bankruptcy Resources > Filing for Bankruptcy without an
Attorney

Emails updates RSS

Filing for Bankruptcy Without an Attorney

Print Share FAQs

Filing for Bankruptcy Without an Attorney

Credit Counseling | Legal Services | Foreclosure | Petition Preparers

Corporations and partnerships must have an attorney to file a bankruptcy case. Individuals, however, may represent themselves in bankruptcy court. While individuals can file a bankruptcy case without an attorney or "pro se", it is extremely difficult to do it successfully.

Debtors must list all property and debts in their bankruptcy schedules. If a debt is not listed, it is possible the debtor will not be discharged. (List of the documents [including schedules] that debtors must file are:

Federal Courts Rules & Procedures Judges & Judgeships Statistics
Forms & Fees Court Records Educational Resources News
Federal Courts

Understanding the Federal Courts Judicial Conference of the United States Bankruptcy
Bankruptcy Basics

Bankruptcy Forms

Bankruptcy Filing Fees

Interim Procedures – Chapter 7 Fee Waivers

Credit Counseling and Debtor Education Courses

Administrative Expense Multiplier Bankruptcy Fraud and Abuse Foreclosures
Bankruptcy Administrators

Building New Credit Habits

CHAPTER IV

As the saying goes, "if you do what you always did, you'll get what you always got". To build new credit, you must replace your credit-damaging spending habits with some new, better ones. Otherwise, you'll end up back where you've worked so hard to get away from.

Gone are the days of charging things you can't afford, making minimum-only payments, and skipping credit card bills on time, preferably in full.

Dos and Don'ts of Using Credit Wisely

Charging Only What You Can Afford

Five Ways to Build a Good Credit History

Remember, what you used to do with credit cards leads to bad credit. Get better habits and watch you credit improve.

PAY EVERYTHING ON TIME

Even if a payment isn't regularly listed on our credit report, it can eventually wind up there if you fall behind on payments. Avoid delinquencies on any accounts, even small ones like library fines, school lunch and medical bills. More businesses are using collection agencies to follow up on their unpaid customer accounts. If one of your accounts lands in the hands of a debt collector, it goes on your credit report for seven years, ruining the progress you've made so far.

REPLACE BAD CREDIT WITH GOOD CREDIT

If practice really does make you perfect, the next step is to put your good credit habits into practice. Your bad credit won't improve until you show your creditors that you have what it takes to build a good score. That means charging only what you can afford and paying your bill on time each month. During this rebuilding period, don't take on too many credit cards because it can get hard to manage your balances and payments. One or two credit cards are plenty to get you started.

START BY GETTING NEW CREDIT

If bad credit has left you without any credit cards, the first step is getting one. Many people swear off credit cards after bad credit, but that's not the way to go. Using a credit card the right way helps you establish a positive payment history.

If your credit score is low, you'll have a hard time getting approval from a major bank. Fortunately, you still have some options:

Cooperatives

Credit Union

Department Store or Gas Credit Car

Secured Personal Loans Secured Credit Card Your Local Bank Branch Find Credit Cards for Bad Credit Scores

Be careful when you apply for new credit. Make sure you don't put in too many credit
applications. It will affect your credit score, making it harder to get approved for new credit.

Watch out for bad credit cards that prey on people with bad credit. These credit cards often have high interest rates and extremely high fees that make credit unaffordable. A lot of people find themselves right back in debt with damaged credit after trying to rebuilt with one of these types of credit card targeting people with bad credit.

You should also avoid prepaid credit cards. While you can get a prepaid credit card regardless of
your credit history, they don't report to credit bureaus so using one won't help your credit.

If your credit card application is denied, don't rush out and put in more credit card applications. Instead, wait to get the letter in the mail that tells you the specific reasons you were denied. Your being turned down may have nothing to do with your credit score, but could be related to another factor, like your income.

REESTABLISHING YOUR CREDIT

Repairing your credit – getting rid of the negative credit report information and caught up on past due bills – will raise your credit score some. To increase you score to a level high enough to get loan approval and better interest rates (which happens to be above 720 these days), you'll have to rebuild your bad credit. That means providing that you can handle credit responsibly. Getting started might be difficult, but once you build momentum, you'll be coasting your way to a good credit score.

There are banks that are willing to help you reestablish your credit standing and your empirica by allowing a credit line by using a savings account or any guarantee instrument in their bank thus you'll have the opportunity to start using credit lines and proving and improving your ability to pay back on time. You will find many banks in the United States of American and Puerto Rico and I will give you the names of the banks – HR Mortgage, Hispania Mortgage and GuraCoop. I do not trust any of these credit companies or banks that are willing to allow you to have a credit line or any credit with their companies at an unbelievable rate which will put you in a situation worse than the one started out with.

The following is a list of banks and credit companies that willing to help you out with your credit situation:

Banco Popular - San Juan Chase in the USA Coopertiva Saulo Sanchez

There are other entities which will help you increase your empirica. The Chinese and German (Deutschland) should have their own system to develop the reestablishment of good credit standing for those affected in the recent worldwide economic situation of the last few years.

CHAPTER V

WHAT IS CREDIT REHABILITATION?

It is possible to improve your credit. Legitimate processes require time, effort, and adherence to a plan for repayment of debts there is no instant remedy. Yet, it is possible to undertake this task independently, without an attorney if you wish. The rewards for improving creditworthiness include everything from qualifying for car loans and mortgages to lower insurance premiums and job offers.

Now that you are convinced of merits of repairing credit and are ready to work, you may be wondering how to get started.

REPAIR YOUR CREDIT

† Recognize that you cannot remove negative information from your credit report if the information is accurate and timely.

† Request an investigation of information in your credit file, free of charge, so that you can check for inaccuracies or omissions.

† For any company that takes the adverse action against you, such as denying a credit, insurance or employment application, request a free annual credit report. Request the report within 60 days of obtaining your first notice of the action taken against you.

† Request you free annual credit report each year if you are unemployed and plan to seek work within 60 days, or if you receive welfare, notice inaccurate information on our credit report that is due to a fraud committed against you, or if you are a victim of identity theft.

† Each of the major national credit reporting agencies – Experian, Equifax, and Trans Union – is required to provide a free annual credit report each year to consumers who request them. Request by website, phone, or mail. Be careful not to make the request online through a service claiming to provide a free credit report but that tacks on a monthly credit-monitoring fee.

† Dispute mistakes and stale (outdated) items included in the credit file. Credit reporting agencies that receive updates and corrections are required to update incomplete, inaccurate, and outdated information, or they are subject to fines, sanctions and penalties.

† Put everything to credit reporting agencies in writing (letter form) and include copies of copies of supporting documents. Retain originals. Send letters by certified mail so that you have proof of receipt. Attach a notated copy of your credit report.

† Items you dispute must be investigated, and the credit reporting agency must report results of the investigation in writing, once completed, with a free copy of your credit report if the dispute creates a change in the report. Corrected copies of your credit report can be sent to those who recently requested and/or obtain it.

† If your dispute is unresolved by investigation, you may request inclusion of a statement of the dispute in your credit report. You may request that anyone who recently received the report obtain an updated copy.

† Request that items that are negative and accurate be removed after requisite waiting periods.

These may include bankruptcies, judgments, and criminal convictions.

DEBT SETTLEMENT

Credit card debt – along with other forms of unsecured debt – is a mounting problem in the United States. More people are in over their heads than ever if you're one of them, it's important to realize that you're not alone, and that help is available. At the same time, it is critical to be aware of the many unscrupulous credit counseling agencies and other organizations that will gladly pocket your hard- earned cash – without providing any real counseling or assistance. Whether you're considering bankruptcy or simply want to learn more about debt elimination.

IN TOO DEEP? YOU HAVE PLENTY OF OPTIONS

One of the worst things you can do when it comes to mounting credit card debt is ignore the problem. Being proactive is of the essence; fortunately, there are many great avenues to pursue. Familiarize yourself with the various options, as outlined below:

† **Work with your creditors** – Many times, simply contacting your various creditors and explaining the circumstances can garner you reduced interest rates and other benefits. Making such contact without knowing how to proceed, though, can result in failure.
† **Debt Consolidation** – A very popular option among many debt-saddled individuals is debt consolidation. Weeding through the various programs that are available can be daunting.
† **Arbitration** – When things come to a head with a credit card company or another creditor, arbitration can help cool things down and level the playing field a bit, too. Arbitration is a great way to settle debts.

You will need:

† Trans Union, Equifax, Experian Scores
† Daily Credit Monitoring & Alerts
† Your Scores Delivered in Seconds (After verification of your identity, your scores are available for secure online delivery in seconds).

Why do I need to check my Credit Score? A good credit score is your passport to competitive interest rates for mortgages, cars, credit card offers, job offers, insurance premiums and more. A strong score is worth money because it saves you in excess cost.

DEBT SETTLEMENT

Have more debt than you can possibly pay? Before filing for personal bankruptcy, consider seeing if your creditors are willing to settle your debt for less than you actually owe. Debt settlement attorneys can help you rid yourself of debt, often for pennies on the dollar.

CCCS

CCCS stands for Consumer Credit Counseling Services. Every counseling office in the CCCS network offers a common set of services, including financial education, budgeting assistance, and Debt Management Plans.

WHAT IS….

Consumer Credit Counseling Services

Being a CCCS means the agency is a member of the NFCC. That carries extra guarantees of quality like accreditation by the CDA, counselor certification, and negotiated concessions from creditors.

All CCS agencies are 501(c)(3) nonprofit organizations, and most will offer other guarantees of nonprofit creditability, like membership in the Better Business Bureau. Springboard has maintained an A rating with the BBB since 1983.

Some agencies, like Springboard, offer HUD-approved housing counseling services, though all
CCCS agencies may not offer the same level of housing counseling.
HISTORY OF CONSUMER CREDIT COUNSELING SERVICES
The NFCC was founded as the National Foundation for Consumer Credit in 1951. Credit cards were still a very new financial product then, and the NFCC was founded to promote awareness of credit and financial literacy.

Very soon, credit counseling emerged as a part of the NFCC's nonprofit service. Individual CCCS offices sprang up around the country, including Springboard, which began in 1974 as Consumer Credit Counseling Service of the Inland Empire.

These CCCS offices were a kind of franchise. Independently operated, their common membership in the NFCC gave them access to counselor certification, educational materials, public relations support, a point of centralized negotiation with the creditors, and more.

Credit counseling became so central to the NFCC that they changed their name from the

National Foundation for Consumer Credit to the National Foundation for Credit Counseling.

In 1993, the Association of Independent Consumer Credit Counseling agency (AICCCA) was founded. AICCCA offered an alternative to the NFCC, and brought a focus on new technologies that allowed counseling by phone and eventually the internet, allowing credit counseling agencies to reach a wider geographical area.

Some CCCS agencies, like Springboard, belong to both the NFCC and AICCA. In order to allow nationwide credit counseling without confusion, we needed a new identity. The agency changed its name to Springboard, but as an NFCC member, we are still CCCS of the Inland Empire.

Credit Counseling Sessions

Consumers who call a CCCS are given access to a confidential, non-judgmental consultation with a certified counselor. This counseling session takes 45 to 90 minutes, and involves a comprehensive review of one's debt and personal finances. The counselor offers expert advice along with a workable budget based on the client's unique financial situation. By tailoring our advice to the client's circumstances, we can offer a realistic plan for paying down debt, increasing savings, and improving the client's financial situation.

Because the counseling session is free of charge and carries no obligation, we urge any consumer with financial concerns or mounting debt to take advantage of this nonprofit community service.

DEBT MANAGEMENT PLANS

Any CCCS agency can offer a Debt Management Plan (DMP) that consolidates the consumer's unsecured credit and debt payments into one new convenient monthly payment. This may offer many advantages:

† A simple payment of all of your creditors

† Total monthly payment amount may reduced
† Interest rates may be lowered
† DMP designed to pay off debt in 3-5 years
† Budgeting advice and support for every client

Considering a typical credit card is designed to take 20-30 years to pay off at the minimum monthly payment, a DMP from a CCCS agency eliminates debts much faster than traditional methods.

Even without a DMP, credit counseling clients benefit from a free, confidential session that provides them with a workable budget and expert advice on managing personal finances and reducing debt over time.

CHAPTER VI

ADDITIONAL SERVICES Bankruptcy Certificates Foreclosure Assistance Reverse Mortgage Counseling

This company will allow your accounts to be charged off (written off as loss).

WHAT IS....

Empirica Credit Score

   †   Fico Credit Score
   †   **Empirica Credit Score**
   †   Beacon Credit Score
   †   Fair Isaac Credit Score

Each credit bureau has a different type of credit score. An Empirica Score is a credit score used by Trans Union credit bureau. Empirica subscribes to the Fair Isaac's FICO model of scoring and then they integrate their own version of a person's FICO score. The Trans union Empirica score is on a scale of 150 to 934.

WHAT IS ....

Credit Scores

   †   Fico Credit Score
   †   Empirica Credit Score

† Beacon Credit Score
† Fair Isaac Credit Score

Along with the credit report, lenders can purchase a credit score based on the information in the credit report. A credit score is calculated by using many types of information that are on your credit report at that agency. By comparing this information patterns in hundreds of thousands of past credit reports, the credit score identifies your level of future credit risk.

In order for a credit score to be calculated on your credit report, there must be a credit history. This means, the credit report must contain at least one account which has been open for six months or greater. In addition, the credit report must contain at least one account that has been updated in the past six months. Since the information on your credit report is the base for calculating a credit score, this ensures that there is enough information to calculate an accurate number.

WHAT IS ...

Beacon Credit Score

† Fico Credit Score
† Empirica Credit Score
† **Beacon Credit Score**
† Fair Isaac Credit Score

Each credit bureau has a different type of credit score. A Beacon Score is a credit score used by Equifax credit bureau. Equifax subscribes to the Fair Isaac's FICO model of scoring and then they integrate their own version of a person's FICO score. The Equifax Beacon credit score is on a scale of 340 to 820.

Equifax markets their credit score under the name Score Power. They've partnered with Fair Isaac, so they use the FICO score, and the Fico score uses a scale from 300 to 850 where 661 or 681 is very good. The concept of credit scores started back in 1956 with two men names Bill Fair and Earl Isaac. Fair, a mathematician, and Isaac, an engineer, fund the Fair Isaac Company; otherwise, known to us today, as the

FICO score. The credit system has had standardized the way the financial industry extends credit.

WHAT IS ...

Experian Credit Report

† Equifax Credit Report
† **Experian Credit Report**
† Trans Union Credit Report
    ✓ Discover the power of Experian Credit Manager
    ✓ Put your best foot forward Sample Credit Report
    ✓ Sample Credit Center
    ✓ Sample Monitoring Alert
    ✓ Sample Plus Score Simulator
    ✓ Lenders frequently use credit scores to determine your credit worthiness. Experian Credit Manager gives you the power to see you PLUS Score and Experian Credit Report as often as you like.
    ✓ Receive unlimited access to your Experian Credit Report as a full member so you can make sure everything is current and accurate.
    ✓ Get a real-time look at your PLUS Score and understand how lenders may view your credit risk.
    ✓ Use the PLUS Score Simulator to see how different factors affect your score.

Your early warning system for fraud and identity theft

Experian Credit Manager gives you peace of mind by scanning your credit report daily and alerting you of critical changes in your credit report that may indicate possible fraudulent activity. By daily monitoring to notify you of fraudulent activity, new inquiries, new accounts, late payments, and more.

Get alerted of critical changes to your credit report with notifications via email.

Take charge of your credit health

Work directly with Experian to catch mistakes on your credit report that may be affecting your credit rating. Get exclusive tips and tools to help you better understand the importance of your credit history.

Access to credit dispute forms and tips to quickly correct mistakes that could be hurting your credit rating

Get valuable credit tools and calculator to make your credit work for you.

Try Experian Credit Manager for 30 days and experience for yourself how credit management can change your financial life.

About Credit Report Offers

Credit Bureaus Provides a Credit Report annually. Is there Still a Need to Buy A Credit Report? (PRWEB) updated January 19, 2005 – Under the Fair and Accurate Credit Transactions Act, the

three national credit bureaus, Equifax, Experian, and TransUnion, must provide a free, annual credit report to every consumer upon request. A national roll-out of the free reports began December 1, 2004. Depending on where you live, you may not be eligible for the Credit Report until September 1, 2005.

If you're looking to make a major purchase and are not yet eligible to receive your Credit Report, you may wish to purchase a credit report online. Purchasing an online credit report can provide you with instant access to your credit information so that you can immediately react to any accuracy. Each credit bureau agency may carry different information on your credit report, so it is often recommended

that you check all three credit reports. annualCreditReport.com allows you to do just that, instantly and online (so long as you correctly answer questions about your credit history for authentication purposes).

Credit bureaus are not required to provide you with a Credit score, which is a major determining factor when you're buying or refinancing a home. Each of the major credit bureaus have provided the option of purchasing your credit score online during the Credit Report process so that you can quickly review your entire credit information. Each credit bureau may reflect a different score for you, so it is a good idea to check all three credit scores. They also offer an easy vehicle to initiate credit disputes so that you can correct incorrect credit information while you're viewing the report. Accurate credit information is particularly important when you're trying to obtain a competitive interest rate and inaccurate credit information is lowering your credit score.

Featured Products

Each of the three major credit bureaus offer a service they often refer to as a credit monitoring service, which allows you to check your credit report and score anytime you want, and even alerts you by e-mail if there is a significant change to your credit information. Credit monitoring services are especially popular with anyone who has ever been or has a fear of becoming a victim of fraud. The U.S. Federal Trade Commission says it takes 12 months, on average, for a victim of identity theft to notice the crime. A credit monitoring service will alert you, usually daily or weekly, to changes in your credit – helping you to stop the theft before it gets out of control.

DON'T USE A CREDIT REPAIR CLINIC

Steer clear of credit repair clinics – you can repair your credit yourself

If you want to clean up your credit file, steer clear of credit repair clinics. These companies claim they can fix your credit, qualify you for a loan, or get you a credit card. But you shouldn't have to pay for these services: these companies can legally do only what you can easily do yourself. And some of them use questionable tactics that can land you in hot water.

Some Credit Repair Clinics Use Illegal Tactics

Some credit repair clinics use practices that are fraudulent, deceptive, and even illegal. For example, credit repair clinics have been caught:

†   Stealing the credit files of Social Security numbers of people who are under 18 or have died, and substituting these for the files of people with poor credit histories, and

†   Advising clients to create a new identity by applying for a IRS Employer Identification number (EIN), a nine-digit number that resembles a Social Security number, and using it instead of their Social Security number to apply for credit – which is illegal.

You Can Repair Your Credit For Free

Even if a credit repair company is legitimate, it can't do anything for you that you can't do yourself. What the company will do, however, is charge you between $250 and $5,000 for their unnecessary services.

What Credit Repair Companies Claim to Do

Here's what accredit repair companies claim they can do – and how to do it yourself:

Remove incorrect information from your credit file. You can do that yourself under the Fair Credit
Reporting Act.

Remove correct, but negative, information from your credit file. Negative items in your credit file can legally stay there for seven years or more (depending on the type of information), as long as they are correct. No one can wave a wand and make them go away.

One credit repair clinic tactic is to challenge every item is a credit file – negative, positive, or neutral – with the hope of overwhelming the credit bureau into removing information without verifying it. However, credit bureaus often dismiss these challenges on the ground that they are frivolous, and a right that credit bureaus have under the Fair Credit Reporting Act. You are better off getting your file and selectively challenging the items that are incomplete or inaccurate.

Even if the credit bureau removes information that a credit bureau had the right to include in your file, it's no doubt only a temporary removal. Most correct information reappears after 30-60 days, because the creditor that first reported the information to the credit bureaus will report it again.

Get outstanding debt balances and court judgment removed from your credit file. Credit repair clinics often advise debtors to pay outstanding debts if the creditor agrees to remove the negative information from your credit file. This is certainly a negotiation tactic you want to consider, but you don't need to pay a credit repair clinic for this advice.

Advise you to get a major credit card. Credit repair clinics can give you a list of banks that offer secured credit cards – credit cards used against a balance you deposit in a bank account. (This is the first step to getting a major credit card if you have bad credit). While this information is helpful in rebuilding credit, it's not worth paying for – you can find this information yourself for little or nothing.

For-profit vs. Nonprofit Credit Repair Companies

The federal Credit Repair Organizations Act prohibits for-nonprofit credit repair clinics from engaging in certain practices and making certain claims about their services. Many states regulate credit repair clinics as well. Some dubious credit repair clinics have tried to get around these regulations by setting themselves up as nonprofits.

Before using any organization that claims to be a nonprofit, carefully check the company's fees, claims about its services, and reputation. Contact the Better Business Bureau (you can find your local BBB at www.bbb.org / http://www.bbb.org and ask if any complaints have been filed against the company. Do the same with your local consumer protection agency. You can verify nonprofit status by contacting the Internal Revenue Services at www.irs.gov / http://www.irs.gov (but just because the company is a nonprofit does not mean it's legitimate).

CREDIT REPAIR: HOW TO HELP YOURSELF

You see the ads in newspapers, on TV, and online. You hear the on the radio. You get fliers in the mail, email messages, and maybe even calls offering credit repair services. They all make the same claim:

"Credit problems? No problem"

"We can remove bankruptcies, judgments, liens, and bad loans from your credit file forever" "We can erase your bad credit – 100% guaranteed"
"Create a new credit identity – legally".

Do yourself a favor and save some money, too. Don't believe these claims; they're very likely signs of a scam. Indeed, attorneys at the Federal Trade Commission, the nation's consumer protection agency, say they've never seen a legitimate credit repair operation making those claims. The fact is there's no quick fix for creditworthiness. You can improve your credit report legitimately, but it takes time, a conscious effort, and sticking to a personal debt repayment plan.

- † Your Rights
- † DIY
- † Reporting Accurate Negative Information
- † Report Credit Repair Fraud
- † Where to Get Legitimate Help

YOUR RIGHTS

No one can legally remove accurate and timely negative information from a credit report. You can ask for an investigation – at no charge to you – of information in your file that you dispute as inaccurate or incomplete. Some people hire a company to investigate for them, but anything a credit repair company can do legally, you can do for yourself at little or no cost. By law:

- † You're entitled to a free credit report if a company takes "adverse action" against you, like denying your application for credit, insurance, or employment. You have to ask for your report within 60 days of receiving notice of the action. The notice includes the name, address, and phone number of the consumer reporting company. You're also entitled to one free report a year if you're unemployed and plan to look for a job within 60 days, if you are on welfare; or if your report is inaccurate because of fraud, including identity theft.

† Each of the nationwide credit reporting companies – Equifax, Experian, and TransUnion – is required to provide you with a free copy of your credit report once every 12 months, if you ask for it. To order, visit annualcreditreport.com or call 1-877-322-8228. You may order reports from each of the three credit reporting companies at the same time, or you can stagger your requests throughout the year.

† It doesn't cost anything to dispute mistakes or outdated items on your credit report.

Both the credit reporting company and the information provider (the person, company, or organization that provides information about you to a credit reporting company) are responsible for correcting inaccurate or incomplete information in your report. To take advantage of all your rights, contact both the credit reporting company and the information provider.

DIY

Step 1: Tell the credit reporting company, in writing, what information you think is inaccurate, include copies (NOT originals) of any documents that support your position. In addition to including your complete name and address, your letter should identify each item in your report that you dispute; state the facts and the reasons you dispute the information, and ask that it be removed or corrected. You may want to enclose a copy of your report, and circle the items in question. Send your letter by certified mail, "return receipt requested", so you can document that the credit reporting company got it. Keep copies of your dispute letter and enclosures.

CHAPTER VII

SAMPLE LETTER

DATE

Your Name
Your Address
City, State, Zip Code

Complaint Department Name of Company Address
City, State, Zip Code

Dear Sir or Madame:

I am writing to dispute the following information in my file. The items I dispute also are circled on the attached copy of the report I received.

This item (identify item (s) disputed by name of source, such as creditors or tax court, and identify type of item, such as credit account, judgment, etc.) is (inaccurate or incomplete) because (describe what is inaccurate or incomplete and why). I am requesting that the item be deleted (or request another specific change) to correct the information.

Enclosed are copies of (use this sentence if applicable and describe an enclosed documentation, such as payment records, court documents) supporting my position. Please investigate this (these) and (delete or correct) the disputed item(s) as soon as possible.

Sincerely,

Your name
Enclosures (list what you are enclosing)

Credit reporting companies must investigate the items you question within 30 days – unless they consider your dispute frivolous. They also must forward all the relevant data you provide about the inaccuracy to the organization that provided the information. After the information provider gets notice of a dispute from the credit reporting company, it must investigate, review the relevant information, and report the results back to the credit reporting company. If the investigation reveals that the disputed information is inaccurate, the information provider has to notify the nationwide credit reporting companies so they can correct it in your file.

When the investigation is complete, the credit reporting company must give you the results in writing, too, and a free copy of your report if the dispute results in a change. If an item is changed or deleted, the credit reporting company cannot put the disputed information back in your file unless the information provider verifies that it's accurate and complete. The credit reporting company also must send you written notice that includes the name, address, and phone number of the information provider. If you ask, the credit reporting company must send notices of any correction to anyone who got your report in the past six months. You also can ask that a corrected copy of your report be sent to anyone who got a copy during the past two years for employment purposes.

If an investigation doesn't resolve your dispute with the credit reporting company, you can ask that a statement of the dispute be included in your file and in future reports. You also can ask the credit reporting company to give your statement to anyone who got a copy of your report in the recent past. You'll probably have to pay for this service.

Step 2: Tell the creditor or other information provider, in writing, that you disputed an item. Include copies (NOT originals) of documents that support your position. Many providers specify an address for disputes. If the provider reports the item to a consumer reporting company, it must include a notice of your dispute. And if the information is found to be inaccurate, the provider may not report it again.

This is an example of the first Credit Repair Dispute Letter in this three letter kit:

DATE

Full Name
Address
Social Security Number

Bureau Name
Address

Dear Sir or Madame:

RE: Company / Name & Account Number

I am writing to dispute the following information in my file. The item I am disputing is also highlighted on the attached copy of the report I received.

I believe this account is inaccurate. Under the Fair Dept. Collection Practice Act, I have a right to request validation and proof from the repositories that these depts. are or are not my obligation. I have requested this information personally from the above referenced company and received no response. I am requesting that the item be deleted or updated to correct the information. I am positive I never signed any agreement authorizing this company to report me as delinquent.

Please investigate this matter and delete the disputed item as soon as possible. Please inform me of any changes, corrections or actions regarding this matter. Please mail me correspondence of the day you receive my request and the day the inquiry is initiated. I am planning on purchasing a new home for my family and I want to clear up any incorrect information before I start the procedure.

Sincerely,

Full name

DATE

Full Name
Address
Social Security Number

Bureau Name
Address

Dear Sir or Madame:

RE: Company Name / Account Number

I recently wrote to you disputing the above mentioned information in my file. The item I am disputing is also highlighted on the attached copy of my credit report.

I have not received the evidence that I requested from your Bureau. This company was not authorized to report me delinquent. I believe this account is inaccurate. Under the Fair Dept. Collection Practice Act, I have a right to request validation and proof from the repositories that these depts. are or are not my obligation. I am requesting that the item be deleted or updated to the correct information. A copy of the authorizing signature should be requested with the investigation. I have requested this information personally, from the above reference company and received no response. Once again, PLEASE FORWARD PROOF of receipt of the authorizing signature and any other evidence you should receive.

Please investigate this matter and delete the disputed item as soon as possible. Please inform me of any changes, corrections or actions regarding this matter. Please mail me correspondence of the day you receive my request and the day the inquiry is initiated. I am planning on purchasing a new home for my family and I want to clear up any incorrect information before I start the procedure.

Sincerely, Your name

DATE

Full Name
Address
Social Security Number

Bureau Name
Address

Dear Sir or Madame:

RE: Company Name / Account Number

I recently wrote to you disputing the following information in my file. The item I am disputing is also highlighted on the attached copy of my credit report.

I believe this account is inaccurate. Under the Fair Dept Collection Practices Act, I have a right to request validation and proof from the repositories that these depts are or are not my obligation. I am requesting that the item be deleted or updated to the correct information. A copy of the authorizing signature should be requested with the investigation. I have requested this information personally, from the above reference company and received no response. Please forward the proof of receipt of the authorizing signature and any other evidence you should receive.

Please investigate this matter and delete the disputed item as soon as possible. Please inform me of any changes, corrections or actions regarding this matter. Please mail me correspondence of the day you receive my request and the day the inquiry is initiated. I am planning on purchasing a new home for my family and I want to clear up any incorrect information before I start the procedure.

Sincerely, Your name

Reporting Accurate Negative Information

When negative information in your report is accurate, only time can make it go away. A credit reporting company can report most accurate negative information for seven years and bankruptcy information for 10 years. Information about an unpaid judgment against you can be reported for seven years or until the statute of limitations runs out, whichever is longer. The seven-year reporting period starts from the date the event took place. There is no time limit on reporting information about criminal convictions; information reported in response to your application for a job that pays more than $75,000 a year, and information reported because you've applied for more than $150,000 worth of credit or life insurance.

The Credit Repair Organization Act

The <u>Credit Repair Organization Act (CROA)</u> makes it illegal for credit repair companies to lie about what they can do for you, and to charge you before they've performed their services. The CROA is enforced by the Federal Trade Commission and requires credit repair companies to explain:

- † Your legal rights in a written contract that also details the services they'll perform
- † Your three day right to cancel without any charge
- † How long it will take to get results
- † The total cost you will pay
- † Any guarantees

What if a credit repair company you hired doesn't live up to its promises? You have some
options. You can:

- † Sue the in federal court for your actual losses or for what you paid them, whichever is more
- † Seek punitive damages – money to punish the company for violating the law
- † Join other people in a class action lawsuit against the company, and if you win, the company has to pay your attorney's fees.

Report Credit Repair Fraud

State Attorneys General

Many states also have laws regulating credit repair companies. If you have a problem with a credit repair company, report it to your local consumer affairs office or to your state attorney general (AG).

Federal Trade Commission

You also can file a complaint with the Federal Trade Commission. Although the FTC can't resolve individual credit disputes, it can take action against a company if there's a pattern of possible law violations. File your complaint online at ftc.gov/complaint or call 1-800-FTC-HELP.

Where to get Legitimate Help

Just because you have a poor credit history doesn't mean you can't get credit. Creditors set their own standards, and not all look at your credit history the same way. Some may look only at recent years to evaluate you for credit, and they may give you credit if your bill-paying history has improved. It may be worthwhile to contact creditors informally to discuss their credit standards.

If you're not disciplined enough to create a budget and stick to it, to work out a repayment plan with your creditors, or to keep track of your mounting bills, you might consider contacting a credit counseling organization. Many are nonprofit and work with you to solve your financial problems. But remember that "nonprofit" status doesn't guarantee free, affordable, or even legitimate services. In fact, some credit counseling organizations – may charge high fees or hide their fees by pressuring people to make "voluntary" contributions that only cause more debt.

Most credit counselors offer services through local offices, online, or on the phone. If possible, find an organization that offers in-person counseling. Many universities, military bases, credit unions, housing authorities, and branches of the U.S. Cooperative Extension Service operate nonprofit credit counseling programs. Your financial institution, local consumer protection agency, and friends and family also may be good sources of information and referrals.

If you're thinking about filling for bankruptcy, be aware that bankruptcy laws require that you get credit counseling from a government-approved organization within six months before you file for bankruptcy relief. You can find a state-by-state list of government-approved organizations at www.usdoj.gov/ust, the website of the U.S. Trustee Program. That's the organization within the U.S. Department of Justice that supervises bankruptcy cases and trustees. Be wary of credit counseling organizations that say they are government-approved, but don't appear on the list of approved organizations.

Reputable credit counseling organizations can advise you on managing your money and debts, help you develop a budget, and offer free educational materials and workshops. Their counselors are certified and trained in the areas of consumer credit, money and debt management, and budgeting. Counselors discuss your entire financial situation with you, and can help you develop a personalized plan to solve your money problems. An initial counseling session typically lasts an hour, with an offer of follow-up sessions.

Credit repair letters are used to dispute credit report mistakes. The Experian, TransUnion and Equifax credit unions compile financial information, but they do no audit its accuracy. The FTC explains that consumers are allowed to check their credit bureau records once per year through a government mandated website (see Resources). People who notice mistakes on any of their reports can write dispute letters to the appropriate bureaus to repair the bad information.

Reason

The three big credit bureaus encourage people to use their online forms for dispute filing. The FTC advises against this because credit repair letters have advantages over online submissions. Each bureau lists s postal address for disputes on its website. Letters can be formatted in an efficient way that lists each mistake and a detailed explanation of the problem. Consumers can enclose copies of their own records for proof, like bank or credit card statements and canceled checks. The postal office will send the letters through certified mail for an extra charge and provide proof of delivery. Credit bureaus have 30 days from the receipt date to handle disputes.

Here's a recommendation that several top analysts agree on: www. DailyTradeAlert.com

Contents

Experian, TransUnion and Equifax are not required to follow up on letters for disputes that appear to be frivolous or unfounded, the Divorcenet.com legal website warns. A credit repair letter lends credibility to claim if it is customized for each credit bureau. The three bureaus sometimes have different information in their records, so referring specifically to the contents of each credit report show that the claims are well researched. Every bit of corroborating evidence enclosed with the letter strengthens the credit repair case, too. The letter should list the consumer's name, address, telephone number and Social Security number. It should clearly request that the listed items checked and removed.

Responses

The U.S. Fair Credit Reporting Act obligates the credit bureaus to reply to disputes once they are investigated, which must be done within 30 days, according to the FTC. The bureaus then send response letters explaining if the disputed items were verified or if they were removed from the report. Erasure is required when a lender does not verify the questionable entry. Every removed entry helps the credit repair effort because the negative information no longer exists.

FYIO (For your information only)

AMG Defendants Settle FTC's Debt Collection Charges
Magistrate Judge Finds that American Indian Tribes Are Subject to FTC Act

The Federal Trade Commission has reached a partial settlement with the principal defendants, in its case against the payday lending operation AMG Services Inc., resolving allegations that the defendants threatened consumers in debt collection calls and violated the Electronic Fund Transfer Act, or EFTA. The agreement bars the settling defendants from using threats of arrest and lawsuits as a tactic for collecting debts, and from requiring all borrowers to agree in advance to electronic withdrawals from their bank accounts as a condition of obtaining credit.

The FTC continues to litigate other charges against the AMG defendants, including allegations that they deceived consumers about the cost of their loans by charging undisclosed charges and inflated fees.

The United States Magistrate Judge V. Cam Ferenbach handed the Federal Trade Commission a significant victory in both this case and its overall crackdown on deceptive payday lenders, finding that these lenders remain within the reach of federal law even if they are affiliated with American Indian Tribes. The Magistrate Judge's report and recommendation is now subject to review by United States District Judge Gloria M. Navarro.

The defendants in the AMG case include automobile racer Scott Tucker, his brother Blaine Tucker, four other individuals, AMG Services, Inc., three other Internet-based lending companies, and six related companies. The FTC alleged that the defendants violated the FTC Act by piling on undisclosed and inflated fees, and by threatening borrowers with arrest and lawsuits in debt collection calls. The FTC also alleged that the defendants violated the Truth in Lending Act ("TILA") by giving inaccurate loan information to borrowers, and that it violated EFTA by requiring consumers to preauthorize electronic withdrawals from their bank account as a condition of obtaining credit. According to documents filed by the FTC, over the last five years, the defendants' deceptive and illegal tactics have generated thousands of complaints to law enforcement authorities. In many cases, the defendants' inflated fees left borrowers with supposed debts of more than triple the amount they borrowed.

One of the AMG defendant's main arguments was that the FTC lacked authority to enforce the FTC Act, TILA, and EFTA against tribes and tribal businesses. But Magistrate Judge Ferenbach concluded that the

FTC Act "gives the FTC the authority to bring suit against Indian Tribes, arms of Indian Tribes, and employees and contractors of arms of Indian Tribes", and likewise found that the FTC has authority to bring the TILA and EFTA claims.

The FTC has sued a number of payday lenders for engaging in unfair and deceptive practices against consumers. The court found that the payday lenders cannot avoid three key federal consumer protection statutes – the FTC Act, the Truth in Lending Act, and the Electronic Fund Transfer Act – simply by aligning themselves with American Indian tribes. The FTC alleged that these other lenders, like AMG Services, have employed deception and other illegal conduct to take advantage of financially distressed consumers seeking these loans.

The Commission voted approving the partial settlement in this matter was 4-0. The parties' agreement is subject to court approval. The FTC filed the proposed permanent injunction for the partial settlement in the U.S. District Court for the District of Nevada on July 8, 2013.

NOTE: Permanent injunctions have the force of law when approved and signed by the District Court judge.

The Federal Trade Commission works for consumers to prevent fraudulent, deceptive, and unfair business practices and to provide information to help spot, stop, and avoid them. To file a complaint in English or Spanish, visit the FTC's online Complaint Assistant or call 1-877-FTC-HELP (1-800-
382-4357). The FTC enters complaints into consumer Sentinel, a secure, online database available to
more than 2,000 civil and criminal law enforcement agencies in the U.S. and abroad. The FTC's website
provides free information on a variety of consumer topics.

CFPB (Consumer Financial Protection Bureau) Bulletin (2013-07)

Date: July 10, 2013
Subject: Prohibition of Unfair, Deceptive, or Abusive Acts or Practices in the Collection of Consumer Debts

Under the Dodd-Frank Wall Street Reform and Consumer Protection Act (Dodd-Frank Act), all covered persons or services providers are legally required to refrain from committing unfair, deceptive, or abusive acts or practices (collectively, UDAAPs) in violation of the act. The Consumer Financial Protection Bureau (CFPB or Bureau) is issuing this bulletin to clarify the contours of that obligation in the context of collecting consumer debts.

This bulletin describes certain acts or practices related to the collection of consumer debt that could, depending on the facts and circumstances, constitute UDAAPs prohibited by the Dodd-Frank Act. Whether conduct like that described in this bulletin constitutes a UDAAP may depend on additional facts and analysis. The examples described in this bulletin are not exhaustive of all potential UDAAs. The Bureau may closely review any covered person or service provider's consumer debt collection efforts for potential violations of Federal consumer financial laws.

A. BACKGROUND

UDAAPs can cause significant financial injury to consumers, erode consumers' confidence, and undermine fair competition in the financial marketplace. Original creditors and other covered persons and service providers under the Dodd-Frank Act involved in collecting debt related to any consumer financial product or service are subject to the prohibition against UDAAPs in the Dodd-Frank Act.

In addition to the prohibition of UDAAPs under the Dodd-Frank Act, the Fair Debt Collection Practices Act (FDCPA) also makes it illegal for a person defined as a "debt collector" from engaging in collections practices.

CHAPTER VIII

UDAAP

"the natural consequence of which is to harass, oppress, or abuse any person in connection with the collection of a debt",[3] to "use any false, deceptive, or misleading representation or means in connection with the collection of any debt."[4] The FDCPA generally applies to third-party debt collectors, such as collection agencies, debt purchasers, and attorneys who are regularly engaged in debt collection. All parties covered by the FDCPA must comply with any obligations they have under the FDCPA, in addition to any obligations to refrain from UDAAPs in violation of the Dodd-Frank Act.

Although the FDCPA's definition of "debt collector" does not include some persons who collect consumer debt, all covered persons and service providers must refrain from committing UDDAAPs in violation of the Dodd-Frank Act.

B. Summary of Applicable Standard for UDDAPs

1. Unfair Acts or Practices

The Dodd-Frank Act prohibits conduct that constitutes an unfair act or practice. An act or practice is unfair when:

1. It causes or is likely to cause substantial injury to consumers;
2. The injury is not reasonably avoidable by consumers; and
3. The injury is not outweighed by countervailing benefits to consumers or to competition.

A "substantial injury" typically takes the form of monetary harm, such as fees or costs paid by consumers because of the unfair act or practice. However, the injury does not have to be monetary. Although emotional impact and other subjective types of harm will not ordinarily amount to substantial injury, in certain circumstances emotional impacts may amount to or contribute to substantial injury. In addition, actual injury is not required; a significant risk of concrete harm is sufficient"

An injury is not reasonably avoidable by consumers when an act or practice interferes with or hinders a consumer's ability to make informed decisions or take action to avoid that injury. Injury caused by transactions that occur without a consumer's knowledge or consent is not reasonably avoidable. Injuries that can only be avoided by spending large amounts of money or other significant resources also may not be reasonably avoidable. Finally, an act or practice is not unfair if the injury it causes or is likely to cause is outweighed by its consumer or competitive benefits.

Established public policy may be considered with all other evidence to determine whether an act or practice is unfair, but may not serve as the primary basis for such determination.

2. Deceptive Acts or Practices

The Dodd-Frank Act also prohibits conduct that constitutes a deceptive act or practice. An act or practice is deceptive when:

1. The act or practice mislead or is likely to mislead the consumer,
2. The consumer's interpretation is reasonable under the circumstances;
3. The misleading act or practice is material.

To determine whether an act or practice has actually misled or is likely to mislead a consumer, the totality of the circumstances is considered. Deceptive acts of practices can take the form of a representation or omission. The Bureau also looks at implied representations, including any implications that statements about the consumer's debt can be supported. Ensuring that claims are supported before they are made will minimize the risk of omitting material information and/or making false statements that could mislead consumers.

To determine if the consumer's interpretation of the information was reasonable under the circumstances when representation target a specific audience, such as older Americans or financially distressed consumers, the communication may be considered from the perspective of a reasonable member of the target audience. A statement or information can be misleading even if not all consumers, or not all consumers in the targeted group, would be misled, so long as a significant minority would be misled. Likewise, if a representation conveys more than one meaning to reasonable consumers, one of which is false the speaker may still be liable for the misleading interpretation. Material information is information that is likely to affect a consumer's choice of, or conduct regarding, the product or service. Information that is likely important to consumers is material.

Sometimes, a person may make a disclosure or other qualifying statement that might prevent consumers from being misled by a representation or omission that, on its own, would be deceptive. The Bureau looks to the following factors in assessing whether the disclosure or other qualifying statement is adequate to prevent the deception: whether the disclosure is prominent enough for a consumer to notice; whether the information is presented in a clear and easy to understand format; the placement of the information; and the proximity of the information to the other claims it qualifies.

3. *Abusive Acts or Practices*

The Dodd-Frank Act also prohibits conduct that constitutes an abusive act or practice. An act or practice is abusive when it:

1. Materially interferes with the ability of a consumer to understand a term or condition of a consumer financial product or service; or

Takes unreasonable advantage of -

(a) A consumer's lack of understanding of the material risks, costs, or conditions of the product or service;

(b) A consumer's inability to protect his or her interests in selecting or using a consumer financial product or service; or

(c) A consumer's reasonable reliance on a covered person to act in his or her interest.

It is important to note that, although abusive acts or practices may also be unfair or deceptive, each of these prohibitions are separate and distinct, and are governed by separate legal standards.

C. Examples of Unfair, Deceptive and/or Abusive Acts or Practices

Depending on the facts and circumstances, the following non-exhaustive list, of examples of conduct related to the collection of consumer debt could constitute UDAAPs. Accordingly, the Bureau will be watching these practices closely.

- † **Collecting or assessing a debt and/or any additional amounts in connection with a debt (including interests, fees, and charges) not expressly authorized by the agreement creating the debt or permitted by law.**
- † **Failing to post payments timely or properly or to credit a consumer's account with payments that the consumer submitted on time and then charging late fees to that consumer.**
- † **Taking possession of property without the legal right to do so.**
- † **Revealing the consumer's debt, without the consumer's consent, to the consumer's employer and/or co-workers.**
- † **Falsely representing the character, amount, or legal status of the debt.**
- † **Misrepresenting that a debt collection communication is from an attorney.**
- † **Misrepresenting that a communication is from a government source or th at the source of the communication is affiliated with the government.**
- † **Misrepresenting whether information about a payment or nonpayment would be furnished to a credit reporting agency.**
- † **Misrepresenting to consumers that their debts would be waived or forgiv en if they accepted a settlement offer, when the company does not, in fact, forgive or waive the debt.**

† **Threatening any action that is not intended or the covered person or service provider does not have the authorization to pursue, including false threats of lawsuits, arrest, prosecution, or imprisonment for non-payment of a debt.**

Again, the obligation to avoid UDAAPs under the Dodd-Frank Act is in addition to any obligations that may arise under the FDCPA. Original creditors and other covered persons and service providers involved

in collecting debt related to any consumer financial product or service are subject to the prohibition against UDAAPs in the Dodd-Frank Act. The CFPB will continue to review closely the practices of those engaged in the collection of consumer debts for potential UDAAPs, including the practices described above. The Bureau will use all appropriate tools to assess whether supervisory, enforcement, or other action may be necessary.

Prohibited Conduct for Collection Efforts

† **Hours for phone contact:** contacting consumers by telephone outside of the hours of 8:00 a.m. to 9:00 p.m. local time
† **Failure to cease communication upon request:** communication with consumers in any way (other than litigation) after receiving written notice that said consumer wishes no further communication or refuses to pay the alleged debt, with certain exception, including advising that collection efforts are being terminated or that the collector intends to file a lawsuit or pursue other remedies where permitted.
† **Causing a telephone to ring or engaging any person in telephone conversation repeatedly or continuously:** with intent to annoy, abuse, or harass any person at the called number
† **Communicating with consumers at their place of employment:** after having been advised that this is unacceptable or prohibited by the employer,
† **Contacting consumer known to be represented by an attorney**
† **Communicating with consumer after request for validation has been made:** communicating with the consumer or the pursuing collection efforts by the debt collector *after* receipt of a consumer's written request for verification of a debt made within the 30 day

validation period (or for the name and address of the original creditor on a debt) and *before* the debt collector mails the consumer the requested verification or original creditor's name and address

† **Misrepresentation or deceit:** misrepresenting the debt or using deception to collect the debt, including a debt collector's misrepresentation that he or she is an attorney or law enforcement officer

† **Publishing the consumer's name or address:** on a "bad debt" list

† **Seeking unjustified amounts,:** which would include demanding any amounts not permitted under an applicable contract or as provided under applicable law

† **Threatening arrest or legal action:** that is either not permitted or not actually contemplated

† **Abusive or profane language:** used in the course of communication related to the debt

† **Communication with third parties:** revealing or discussing the nature of debts with third parties (*other than the consumer's spouse or attorney.* (Collection agencies are allowed to contact neighbors or co-workers but only to obtain location information, disreputable agencies often harass debtors with a "block party" or "office party" where they contact multiple neighbors or co-workers telling them they need to reach the debtor on an urgent matter.)

† **Contact by embarrassing media,:** such as communication with a consumer regarding a debt by post card, or using any language or symbol, other than the debt collector's address, on any envelope when communicating with a consumer by use of the mails or by telegram, except that a debt collector may use his business name if such name does not indicate that he is in the debt collection business.

† **Reporting false information on a consumer's credit report:** or threatening to do so in the process of collection.

Required Conduct

The Act requires debt collectors to do the following (among other requirements):

† **Identify themselves and notify the consumer,** in every communication, that the communication is from a debt collector, and in the initial communication that any information obtained will be used to effect collection of the debt.

† **Give the name and address of the original creditor:** (company to which the debt was originally payable) upon the consumer's written request made within 30 days of receipt of the § 1692g notice.

† **Notify the consumer of their right to dispute the debt (Section 805):** in part or in full, with the debt collector. The 30-day "§1692g" notice is required to be sent by debt collectors within five days of the initial communication with the consumer, though in 2006 the definition of the "initial communication" was amended to exclude "a format pleading in a civil action" for purposes of triggering the §1992g notice, complicating the matter where the debt collector is an attorney or law firm. The consumer's receipt of this notice starts the clock running on the 30- day right to demand verification of the debt from the debt collector.

† **Provide verification of the debt:** if a consumer sends a written dispute or request for verification within 30 days of receiving the §1992g notice, then the debt collector must either mail the consumer the requested verification information **or** cease collection efforts altogether. Such asserted disputes must also be reported by the creditor to any credit bureau that reports the debt. Consumers may still dispute a debt verbally or after the thirty–day period has elapsed, but doing so waives the right to compel the debt collector to produce verification of the debt. Verification should include at a minimum the amount owed and the name and address of the original creditor.

† **File a lawsuit in a proper venue:** If a debt collector chooses to file a lawsuit, it may only be in a place where the consumer lives or signed the contract. Note, however, that this does not prevent the debt collector from being sued in other venues for violating the Act, such as when the consumer moves outside the venue and a letter demanding payment is forwarded to the new address, even if the debt collector is unaware of such a change in residence.

Guidance on UDAAP

What is Unfair?

† **UNFAIRNESS** means the act or practice:
† Causes or is likely to cause substantial injury to consumers
† Which is not reasonably avoidable by consumers; and
† Such substantial injury is not outweighed by countervailing benefits to consumers or to competition.

Examples of Unfair Practices

† Refusing to release a lien after consumer makes final payment on mortgage.
† Dishonoring credit card convenience checks without notice.
† Processing payments for companies engaged in fraudulent activities
† Misrepresentation about loan terms

What is Deceptive?

† A representation, omission, act or practice is deceptive when
  - The representation, omission, act, or practice misleads or is likely to mislead the consumer;
  - The consumer's interpretation of the representation, omission, act, or practice is reasonable under the circumstances; and
  - The misleading representation, omission, act, or practice is material

The Four P'S Of Clear and Conspicuous

▪ **PROMINENCE**: Is it big enough for consumers to notice and read?
▪ **PRESENTATION:** Is wording and format easy for consumers to understand
▪ **PLACEMENT:** Is it where consumers will look?
▪ **PROXIMITY:** Is it near the claim that it qualifies?

CHANGES FROM DODD-FRANK

Section 1031 of Dodd-Frank

- The Bureau may take enforcement action to prevent
  - A covered person or service provider
  - From committing or engaging in an unfair, deceptive, or abusive act or practice under Federal Law
  - In connection with any transaction with a consumer for a consumer financial product or service.
- Added the concept of "abusive" to UDAP to make UDAAP What is Abusive?
- Something that materially interferes with the ability of a consumer to understand a term or condition of the product or service; or
- Takes unreasonable advantage of:
- A lack of understanding on the part of the consumer about the risks, costs, or conditions of the product or service,
- The inability of the consumer to protect the interests of the consumer in selecting or using the product or service; or
- The reasonable reliance by the consumer on a covered person to act in the interests of the consumer

Complaints

- Required by Section 1034 of Dodd-Frank
- Timely response required by the regulators to consumer complaints or inquiries
  - ✓ Including any follow-up actions, and
- A duty by the regulated institutions to respond to the Bureau
- CFPB has complaint database online

UDAAP and Complaint Process

- Consumer complaints play a key role in the detection of unfair, deceptive, or abusive practices.
- Those complaints can indicate weaknesses the institution's compliance management system, such as
  - Training,

- Internal controls, or
- Monitoring.
- While the absence of complaints does not ensure that unfair, deceptive, or abusive practices are not occurring, complaints may be one indication of UDAAPs.
  - For example, the presence of complaints alleging that consumers did not understand the terms of a product or service may be a red flag indicating that examiners should conduct a detailed review of the relevant practice.
- When reviewing complaints against an institution, examiners are supposed to consider complaints against
  - Subsidiaries,
  - Affiliates, and
  - Third parties

Regarding the products and services offered through the institution or using the institution's name.

- Examiners may also determine whether an institution itself receives, monitors, and responds to complaints filed against subsidiaries, affiliates, and third parties.
- Examiners should consider the context and reliability of complaints;
  - Every complaint does not indicate violation of law.
- When consumers repeatedly complaint about an institution's product or service, examiners may flag the issue for possible further review.
  - Even a single substantive complaint may raise serious concerns that would warrant further review.
  - Complaints that allege, for example misleading or false statements, or missing disclosure information, may indicate possible unfair, deceptive, or abusive acts or practices needing review.

High-Risk Complaint Types

- Complaints that may indicate possible UDAAPs include:
  - Misleading or false statements
  - Missing disclosures or information

- Undue or excessive fees
- Inability to reach customer service
- Previously undisclosed or unauthorized charges

Risk Areas

- The areas with the greatest potential for unfair or deceptive acts or practices include:
  - Advertising and solicitations
  - Account and loan disclosures
  - Servicing and collections
  - Managing and monitoring of third-party service providers
  - Consumer Complaints

ENFORCEMENT

Enforcement Action

- The CFPB's first public enforcement action was an order requiring a major institution to
  - Refund approximately $140 million to two million customers and
  - Pay an additional $25 million penalty.
- The CFPB said that their action resulted from an examination that identified deceptive marketing tactics used by the institution's vendors

Allegations

- That consumers were pressured or misled into paying for "add-on products" such as payment protection and credit monitoring when they activated their credit cards.
- That consumers with low credit scores or low credit limits were offered these products by call- center vendors when they called to have their new credit cards activated.
- That as part of the alleged tactics used to sell these add-on products, consumers were misled by being led to believe that the product would improve their credit scores and would help them increase the credit limit on their credit card.

- That consumers were deceived by not always told that buying the product was optional or told they were required to purchase the product in order to receive full information about it, but that they could cancel the product if they were not satisfied.
  - Many of these consumers later had difficulty canceling
- That consumers were misled about eligibility because some call center representatives marketed and sold the product to ineligible unemployed and disabled consumers. Despite paying the full fees, they could not get all the benefits of payment protection.
- That consumers were misinformed about cost by being led to believe that they would be enrolling in a free product rather than making a purchase; and
- Where reenrolled without their consent, automatically billed for the product and often having trouble cancelling the product when they called to do so.

Guidance on Marketing Add-on Products

- CFPB Bulletin 2012-06
  http://files.consumerfinance.gov/f/201207_cfpb_marketing_of_credit_card_addon_product.pdf
- Marketing materials
- Compensation
- Scripts
- Compliance Programs

Relationship to Other Laws

- An unfair, deceptive, or abusive act or practice may also violate other federal or state laws.
  - For example, pursuant to the TILA, creditors must "clearly and conspicuously" disclose the costs and terms of credit. An act or practice that does not comply with these provisions of TILA may also be unfair, deceptive, or abusive.
- Conversely, a transaction that is in technical compliance with other federal or state laws *may nevertheless violate the prohibition against UDAAPs*.

- For example, an advertisement may comply with TILA's requirements, but contain additional statements that are untrue or misleading. In that case, compliance with TILA's disclosure requirements does not insulate the rest of the advertisement from the possibility of being deceptive.

QUESTIONS?

WHAT IS UDAAP AND WHY SHOULD YOU CARE?

WHAT TO DO WHEN YOU BUY A HOUSE WITH A BANK MORTGAGE?

Get your personal paperwork in order, evidence and identification

(a) Driver's license, social security card, passport, etc.
(b) Letter of employment verification, copy of recent pay stubs, any other income evidence
(c) Letters of any explanation of any problems you may had in the past, slow pay of any creditors, any bankruptcy in the past, divorces, legal suits

WHO TO CONTACT FOR THIS MORTGAGE?

▪ Any bank, mortgage company or broker who is willing to take the time to help you, must be a real mortgage bank who has the capital to help you immediately

WHEN TO BUY?

(a) You will know when to buy when you find the property of your interest
(b) When the market allows you to buy according to your need, inside your limitations

(c) The bank will tell you immediately if you qualify or not, then you get ready to do what's necessary to go ahead and stat preparing for the next step

WHO IS BUYING THE PROPERTY?

(a) Is it yourself or are you buying with a spouse or a partner.
(b) If it is more than one person then you need to follow the steps on what to do above. WHY DO YOU WANT TO BUY A PROPERTY?
(a) To live as primary residence, as an income producing property or for your children
(b) In any case above the qualifications are different in every case

WHERE DO YOU BUY YOUR PROPERTY?

(a) It is important to know exactly where you are buying this property regarding the neighborhood
(b) Remember, the value of your property is going to be based on LOCATION, LOCATION AND LOCATION any serious minded realtor will tell you this.

On December 19, 2003, President Bush signed into law the "Servicemembers Civil Relief Act" (SCRA).

This law is a complete revision of the Soldiers' and Sailors' Civil Relief Act (SSCRA).

The SSCRA provided a number of significant protections to servicemembers. These include: staying count hearings if military service materially affects servicemembers' ability to defend their interests; reducing interests to 6% on pre-service loans and obligations; requiring court action before a servicemember's family can be evicted from rental property for nonpayment of rent if the monthly rent is $1,200 or less; termination of a pre-service residential lease; and allowing servicemembers to maintain their state of residence for tax purposes despite military relocations to other states.

The SSCRA was largely unchanged from its enactment in 1940. The SCRA was written to: clarify the language of the SSCRA: to incorporate many years of judicial interpretation of the SSCRA: and to update the SSCRA to reflect new developments in American life since 1940. The new law, SCRA:

(1) Extends the application of a servicemember's right to stay court hearings to administrative hearings. It now requires a court or administrative hearing to grant at least a 90-day stay if requested by the servicemember. Additional stays can be granted at the discretion of the judge or hearing official.

(2) Clarifies the rules on the 6% interest rate cap on pre-service loans and obligations by specifying that interest in excess of 6% per year must be forgiven. The absence of such language in the SSCRA had allowed some lenders to argue that interest in excess of 6% is merely deferred. It also specifies that a servicemember must request this reduction in writing and include a copy of his/ her orders.

(3) Modifies the eviction protection section by precluding evictions from premises occupied by servicemembers for which the monthly rent does not exceed $2,400 for the year 2003 (an increase from the current $1,200). The Act provides a formula to calculate the rent ceiling for subsequent years.

(4) Extends the right to terminate real property leases to active duty soldiers moving pursuant to permanent change of station (PCS) orders or deployment orders of at least 90days. This eliminates the need to request a military termination clause in lease.

(5) Adds a new provision allowing the termination of automobile leases for use by servicemembers and their dependents. Pre-service automobile leases may be cancelled if the servicemember receives orders to active duty for a period of 180 days or more. Automobile leases entered into while the servicemember is on active duty may be terminated If the servicemember receives PCS orders to a location outside the continental United States or deployment orders for a - period of 180 days or more.

(6) Adds a provision that would prevent states from increasing the tax bracket of a nonmilitary spouse who earned income in the state by adding in the service member's military income for the limited purpose of determining the nonmilitary spouse's tax bracket. The practice has had the effect of increasing the military family's tax burden.

Historically, the SSCRA applied to members of the National Guard only if they were serving in a Title 10 status. Effective December 6, 2002, the SSCRA protections were extended to members of the National Guard called to active duty for 30 days or more pursuant to a contingency mission specified by the President of the Secretary of Defense. This continues in the SCRA.

Law and Regulation on UDAP

- Section 5 of the FTC Act
  - Prohibits "unfair or deceptive acts or practices in or affecting commerce."
  - The prohibition applies to all persons engaged in commerce, including banks.
- Regulation AA
  - Complaints
  - Credit Practices Rule
    - o Unfair credit contract provisions
    - o Unfair or deceptive practices involving cosigners
    - o Unfair late charges

Significant Guidance on UDA

- OCC Advisory Letter 2002-3
  - http://www.occ.gov/static/news-issuances/memos-advisory-letters/2002/advisory-letter-2002-3.pdf
- Federal Reserve Guidance for State Chartered Banks dated March 11. 2004
  - http://www.federalreserve.gov/boarddocks/press/bcreg/2004/20040311/attachment.pdf

New mortgage lending rules are going into
effect Friday that aim to put an end to the worst
mortgage lending abuses of the past.

The new rules are designed to take a "back to basics" approach to mortgage lending and lower the risk of defaults and foreclosures among borrowers, according to the Consumer Financial Protection Bureau, which issued the new rules.

"No debt traps. No surprises. No runarounds. These are bedrock concepts backed by our new common-sense rules, which take effect today," said CFPB director Richard Cordray in remarks prepared for a hearing Friday.

Related: Million-dollar housing markets

Mortgage lenders are being asked to comply with two new requirements: The Ability to Repay rule and Qualified Mortgages. Here's how they will impact borrowers:

Ability to Repay

- Lenders must determine that a borrower has the income and assets to afford to make payments throughout the life of the loan. To do so, the lender may look at your debt-to-income ratio, which is how much you owe divided by how much you earn per month, including the highest mortgage payments you would be required to make under the terms of the loan. To calculate your debt-to-income ratio, add up all your monthly obligations— including student loan, credit card and car payments, housing costs, utilities and other recurring expenses—and divide it by your monthly gross income.

Calculator: How much house can you afford?

- In an effort to put an end to no- or low-doc loans, where lenders issue risky mortgages without the necessary financial information, lenders will be required to document and verify an applicant's income, assets, credit history and debt. For borrowers, that means more paperwork and longer processing times.

- Underwriters must also approve mortgages based on the maximum monthly charges you face, not just low "teaser rates" that last only a matter of months, or a year or two, before resetting higher.

Qualified Mortgages

- To make sure you aren't taking on more house than you can afford, your debt-to-income ratio generally must be below 43%. This rule is not absolute. Banks can still make loans to people with debt-to-income ratios that are greater than that if other factors, such as a high level of assets, justify the risk.
- Qualified mortgages cannot include risky features, such as terms longer than 30 years, interest-only payments or minimum payments that don't keep up with interest so your mortgage balance grows.
- Upfront fees and charges cannot add up to more than 3% of the mortgage balance. That includes title insurance, origination fees and points paid to lower mortgage interest rates.

The rules also restrict "steering," or practices that give financial incentives to loan officers or mortgage brokers for pushing people into higher-interest loans that they can't afford—a practice that was all too common leading up to the housing bust, Cordray said.

Related: American dream homes: What you'll pay in 10 cities

"We think the new rules are balanced and well-drawn. They will offer consumers protection without limiting credit to qualified borrowers," said Gary Kalman, the policy director for the Center for Responsible Lending.

Lenders don't seem to be too worried about the new rules, according to Keith Gumbinger of HSH.com, a mortgage information provider. "It's no surprise; everybody has been preparing for the change for months," he said. "Because there will be additional underwriting scrutiny, it could gum up the works initially and slow loan processing, but it's really just the codification of things that are already in place."

A significant factor is what's not in the rules. There's no minimum down payment or credit score requirement.

"[The qualifed mortgage] is not taking a one-size-fits-all approach. It ensures that first time homebuyers can still come to the table," said Kalman.

Related: 5 most and least affordable housing markets

If the rules required a minimum down payment of, say 10% or 20%, it would eliminate many first time buyers who would have a difficult time raising that much cash.

The lack of a credit score requirement will enable lenders to loosen currently tight underwriting standards in the future should conditions warrant, according to Gumbinger. For the moment, most loans will still have to be backed by Fannie Mae and Freddie Mac, and, with a few exceptions, they won't approve applicants with scores below 620.

www.ingramcontent.com/pod-product-compliance
Lightning Source LLC
Chambersburg PA
CBHW021900170526

45157CB00005B/1898